ABORIGINES

Virginia Luling

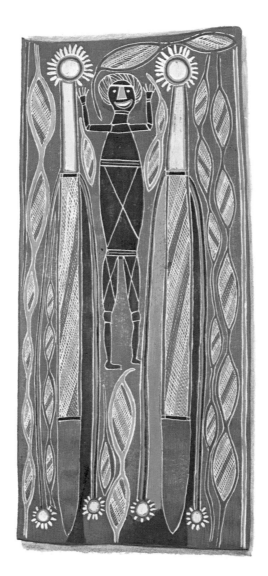

Macdonald Educational

Editor Verity Weston
Assistant Editor June Dale
Design Roland Blunk MSIA
Picture Research Leonora Elford
Production Rosemary Bishop

First published 1979

Macdonald Educational Ltd
Holywell House
Worship Street
London EC2A 2EN
©Macdonald Educational 1979

Artists
Terry Allen Designs Ltd: 6-7, 21
Bryan Evans/Temple Art: 4-5, 8-9
Ron Hayward: 11, 18-19, 22-23, 40,
44-45
Tony Payne: 12-13, 14-15, 17, 26-27,
33, 35, 46
Peter Thornley: 30, 36

ISBN 0-382-06355-4

Published in the
United States by
Silver Burdett Company
Morristown, N.J.

1979 Printing
Library of Congress
Catalog Card No. 79-67165

Contents

From the beginning

"This is our land. It goes back, a long way back, into the Dreamtime, into the land of our Dreaming . . ."
Aboriginal schoolchild

For many ages a dark people has lived in the southern continent of Australia. Until two hundred years ago they had it to themselves. Then the first Europeans arrived, and they called those dark people "Aborigines", meaning "the ones who were there from the beginning".

Aborigines too believed they had been there since the beginning of things. In their Beginning, their legends said, the great Ancestors had walked across the land, and made everything in it: mountains and rivers, plants, animals and people.

They had given the people all they needed and laid down all the rules for the right and proper way to live in their land.

At home in the land

The Aborigines' land was rich in the history of the Ancestors' activities. Every feature of the countryside, every rock and mountain had a name, often linking it to the Ancestor whose activity had made it. There are tens of thousands of place names like this.

Every bit of the country belonged to a small group of relatives called a clan. Although people did build houses, dams, fish weirs, and set traps when hunting, these things did not alter the appearance of the land much.

They lived simply, by fishing, food gathering and hunting.

A complicated world

In spite of that, and although Aborigines had few manufactured things, their life was (and still is) rich and complicated.

It was made up of the relationships of people to each other, and to the land.

Everything – trees, animals, rocks, sun, moon and rainbow – had a meaning and a story.

Part of a wet-season village in Arnhem Land.
The bark-covered huts are raised on stilts so
that smoky fires can be lit under them to protect
against mosquitoes. A hunter gives the lizard he
has caught to his wife to cook, watched by the
half-tame dingo dogs found in every camp. Out
of the way of the dogs are the two men on the
raised platform used for eating and sleeping.

Boys of seven upwards have their own house
(the ground level hut) in which they sleep.

5

The first Australians

Aborigines did not write their history, so the only way to tell what happened to them before the Europeans came is by the things they left behind. Even after thousands of years we can still find tools and weapons; the remains of long ago camp fires, and the meals eaten beside them; and the bones of the people themselves.

Thanks to these things, we know that there have been people in Australia for some 40,000 years.

The first boats

The first Australians arrived from Asia. Forty thousand years ago there was less sea between Australia and the rest of the world than today. But even then, there were some channels up to 80 kilometres wide, so they must have used boats or rafts, some of the first in the world. The people spread over the land and multiplied. By the time the Europeans arrived there were perhaps 300,000 of them.

In this book we shall look at the way Aborigines lived at the time Europeans arrived, although there were many changes in their lives before then. The giant marsupials (mammals who carry their young in a pouch) disappeared, hunted to extinction. And 5,000 years ago the dingo and some new stone tools were brought from Indonesia.

Forest and desert

There were very broadly two patterns of living. One belonged to the coast, the northern tropical forests, and the cooler woodlands of the south and east. There, where food (roots and fish) and water were most plentiful, 90 per cent of the population lived.

The other ten per cent lived on seeds and the wildlife that lived in the deserts of the interior.

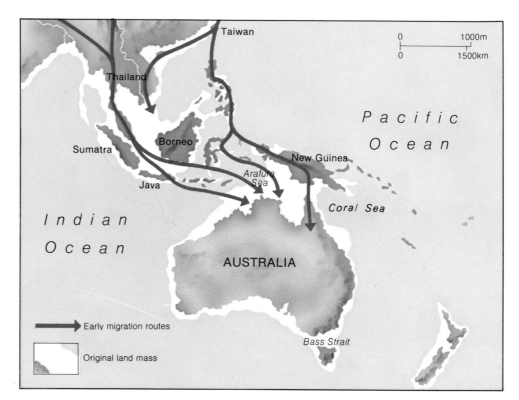

Above We do not know just which routes the ancestors of the Aborigines took to Australia, but the arrows show some possible ones. The map shows the shore-line of 40,000 years ago, during the Ice Age, when so much water was frozen that the seas were emptier.

Left 1 This stone scraper is more than 5,000 years old. **2** A quartzite point about 2,000 years old. **3** This is a flat backed blade.

The more finely shaped tools had more value as gifts, or for use in trade or exchange.

Right Australia has a wide range of climates and environments. Aborigines adapted their lives accordingly.
1 Men from the north-west on a typical raft.
2 Arnhem Land, in the tropical north.
3 In the north-east, houses like these gave protection from the wet season.
4 On the rivers of the south-east, people used bark canoes to travel about in.
5 The Tasmanians are gathering shellfish, one of their main foods.

The map shows the names of only a few of the 500 or more tribes, or language groups.

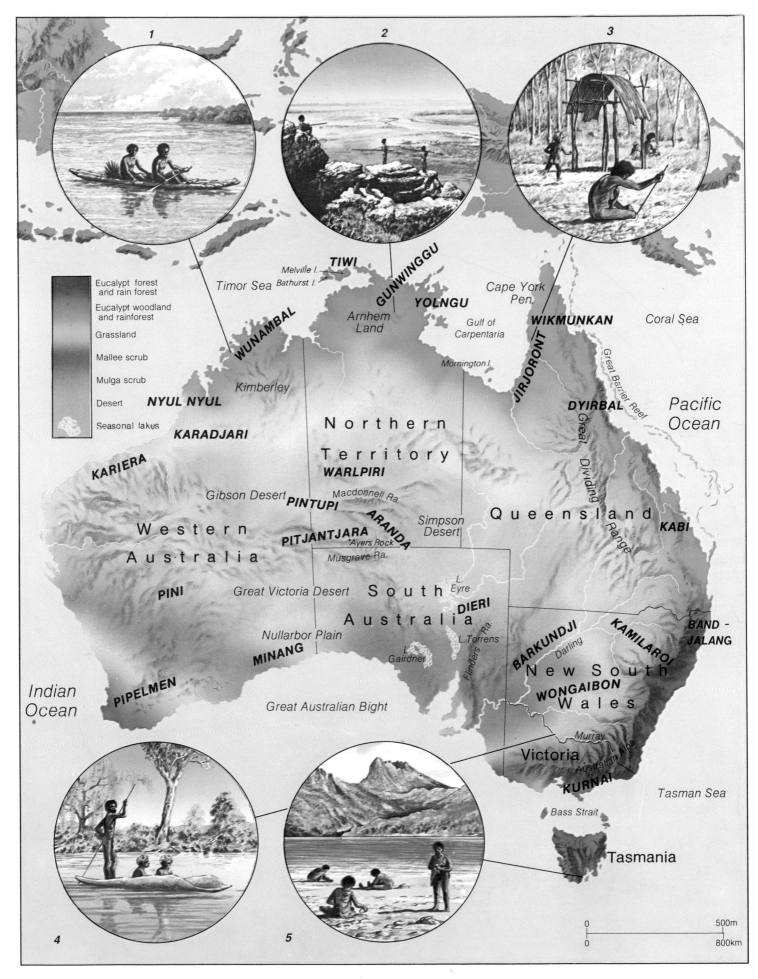

Eucalypt forest and rain forest

Eucalypt woodland and rainforest

Grassland

Mallee scrub

Mulga scrub

Desert

Seasonal lakes

1
2
3

TIWI

Timor Sea

Melville I.
Bathurst I.

GUNWINGGU

YOLNGU

Cape York Pen.

Coral Sea

WUNAMBAL

Arnhem Land

WIKMUNKAN

Gulf of Carpentaria

Mornington I.

JIRJORONT

Great Barrier Reef

DYIRBAL

Pacific Ocean

Kimberley

NYUL NYUL

Northern Territory

KARADJARI

KARIERA

WARLPIRI

Gibson Desert

PINTUPI

Macdonnell Ra.

Queensland

Great Dividing Range

KABI

ARANDA

Simpson Desert

Western Australia

PITJANTJARA

Ayers Rock

Musgrave Ra.

South

L. Eyre

PINI

Great Victoria Desert

Australia

DIERI

KAMILAROI

BAND - JALANG

L.Torrens

Flinders Ra.

BARKUNDJI

Darling

Nullarbor Plain

MINANG

L. Gairdner

New South

WONGAIBON

Wales

Indian Ocean

PIPELMEN

Great Australian Bight

Murray

Victoria

Australian Alps

KURNAI

Tasman Sea

Bass Strait

Tasmania

4
5

0   500m
0   800km

7

Caring for the land

"You people go to all that trouble working and planting seeds, but we don't have to do that. All these things are there for us, the Ancestral Beings left them for us . . ."
Arnhem Land woman

Aborigines lived in harmony with the land around them, disturbing it little when they went fishing, hunting or food gathering.

Those who lived in the north met people from New Guinea or Indonesia and knew from them about farming. They did not copy them, perhaps because that kind of farming did not work well enough in Australia to be worth the trouble.

Aborigines did not keep animals other than the dingo, probably because there were none suitable.

Looking after the land

Aborigines had ways of looking after the land. They put part of some roots back in the ground so that they would grow again the following year. Every year they burnt off the grass, which encouraged the seeds to sprout, and often made hunting kangaroos easier by attracting them to new growth.

Their way of living was probably the one that worked best in their country, until Europeans brought new plants and animals, new methods and machines.

Living in the desert

Finding enough to live on was hardest for those who lived in the desert but there was rarely, if ever, starvation.

In the desert, there is only a short season of rain at the best of times. So there was often a shortage of water near supplies of food.

The important thing in life was to know where all the water sources were, especially those which did not dry up, even in a drought.

For emergency supplies Aborigines shook the dew off leaves in the morning, or found water stored in the roots of trees, or in the belly of a burrowing desert frog.

Left A camp in the desert of Western Australia. The shelters are of dried branches. The woman in front is about to grind wild grass seeds, while her baby rests in one of the dishes. The man on the left strips the bark from a root as he begins to make a new spear. The children are telling stories in the sand.

Below Two calendars which show how two groups of Aborigines in different areas divide the year according to the weather and the food available.

Northern Arnhem Land: coastal forest

Barramirri (Late December – January)
The wet season begins: vegetables are scarce but there are some fruits. People settle in large camps.

Kunmul (January – March)
This is the wet season. Vegetable food is scarce, and travel difficult.

Mirdawarr (Late March – April)
The wet season ends. The first vegetables (especially yams) are eaten, and fish and shellfish.

Tarra tarramiri (April – August)
This is the dry season, and the main hunting season. Wet-season camps break up and people move in small groups.

Rarandarr (September – October)
Hot, dry season, important for ceremonies. Fish are caught by poisoning the remaining pools.

Worlmamirri (October – December)
"The nose of the wet season", damp and hot (30°C) with thunderstorms. Good time for fruits and berries. People gather near permanent water.

Karadjere people: western desert

Manggala (January – February)
The wet season. Fruits and nuts are available. Kangaroos, goannas and fish plentiful. In the desert, pools fill up and travel is easy.

Marul (March – April)
Rains ending. Nuts, mangrove pods, fish and game available.

Pargana (May – August)
Cold SE winds: time to collect honey, dig out goanna, hunt kangaroos.

Wilburu (about September)
Hot SE winds from the desert.

Ladja (October – December)
Very hot. Good time for hunting kangaroos. Water is scarce.

Living on the land

Below This picture was taken recently in Arnhem Land, where people still live close to their old way of life. It shows the kind of house used in the wet season. It is roofed with bark stripped from the trees at the beginning of the season.

For Aborigines, use and ownership were different things. People did not necessarily live on the land they owned, although all the land belonged to one clan or another.

The people moved after the different foods as they came in season. Each group travelled mostly within their own territory along customary paths. At times many people camped together, at others they would split up into groups of one or two families.

Those in the more fertile areas did not need to move far or often. They might stay in one place for months.

In the drier areas inland, the territories were much larger than on the coast. People often only camped a few nights in each place and spent the day travelling and gathering food as they went.

All relations

Each person belonged to a clan, which owned a particular territory. All the clans in one region would speak the same language, follow the same customs, and marry mainly among themselves.

The people in this big grouping would be related to each other. We call this a "tribe" but Aborigines had no special word for it.

Shelter

The kind of shelter people used depended on the region and season. People in the south-east made large and solid houses, some even with stone walls for 12 or more people.

The desert dwellers put up temporary shelters according to the season. In Arnhem Land, in the wet season, they put up solid structures of various kinds; in the dry season they camped in the open or used low wind-breaks.

Left Large bark-covered shelters like this are used in northern Arnhem Land when the rains are at their heaviest. Several families can get inside at once.

Left As the rains become lighter the chief problem is mosquitoes. People make platform houses like this and light fires underneath, so that the smoke keeps the insects off.

Left People living in the desert put up quickly-made windbreaks like these, of spinifex grass. For warmth in the nights, when temperatures can drop below freezing point, each person lights a fire and lies alongside it.

Left In the more fertile south-east, people built more solid houses like this one, which is made of saplings plastered with mud. These houses could be used for months on end.

Left Bark windbreaks like this were used by the islanders of Tasmania, but they too put up solid shelters in winter.

The gatherers

*"Digging into the mud for the rounded roots of the lily,
Piling up the mud as they dig, and washing the roots clean."*
Arnhem Land song

Below A woman of a desert group prepares grass seeds. (Our wheat and barley are simply cultivated grasses.)

She winnows it in her bark tray, shaking the seed in a special way to get rid of the dirt and outer husk. Then she grinds it between two stones, and makes the flour into a small flat loaf which she bakes in the ashes of the fire.

Bottom of page Here are some examples of women's tools. (One of the most important tools was a digging stick, see facing page.)

Aborigines shared equally the tasks of daily living. All men were hunters, on land or sea. Women often had babies or small children with them, so they could not count on travelling far or running fast.

Their work was to collect plant foods, shellfish and small animals and insects. Both men and women knew a great deal about nature and never had difficulty finding food.

Nonetheless, hunters, however skilful, often came home empty-handed. Everyone depended on the women for their main food supply.

Making bread
Women knew how to find and use an enormous number of different plants, both for food and for other things such as medicine or making bags.

In the forested areas the most important were the root vegetables, such as wild yams or water-lilies. In the desert they collected the seeds of grasses, ground them into flour, and made a kind of bread.

People also used the berries and leaves of some plants, or the pith of the stem.

Earth ovens
Women often cooked the men's catch as well as their own. Vegetable foods and small animals were generally baked in the ashes of the fire. For large animals and fish, the people made an earth oven.

They made a pit in the ground, and put a layer of stones heated in the fire at the bottom, and then a layer of green leaves. They jointed the animal, or took out its insides and filled it with hot stones, then laid it on the leaves. They covered it with more leaves and then a thick layer of earth. It would be baked in a few hours.

A valuable grinding stone for grass seeds. Women used them till they wore thin.

Bark dishes (some were made of wood): for everything from seeds to babies.

A bag for carrying food and other things. In English it is called a "dilly bag".

Another type of bag, made of fibres from plant stems or tree-bark.

Above In Arnhem Land people still live largely in the traditional way. This little girl is eating a lizard tail.

Right Digging-stick on shoulder, an Arnhem Land woman returns to camp. The palm kernels on her back must be soaked for three to five days, then pounded, made into loaves, and baked.

Below Six of the hundreds of plants used for food.

Acacia seeds are a source of protein in the desert.

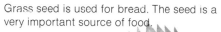

Grass seed is used for bread. The seed is a very important source of food.

Wild yam is an important root vegetable, particularly in the tropical north.

A fruit from the same family as our tomato, very valuable to desert dwellers.

Blue Water Lily: roots and seed pods are eaten in the dry season in Arnhem Land.

The Willow Geebung has a sharp-tasting fruit, eaten in the temperate south.

The hunters

Below Rock paintings often depicted the animals Aborigines hunted. These Arnhem Land paintings are of turtles, dugong and barramundi.

Bottom of page Trapping an emu in Queensland. The hunters made an alleyway of bushes with a net across one end. One man, behind the net, blew on a hollow log to imitate the emu's call. Curious, the big birds came to the sound, and the other hunters came out of hiding and drove them into the net.

Men provided most of the meat. Their main weapon was the spear, with a point of hardened wood or stone. To make it fly further, a hunter used a spear-thrower (or *woomera*). This is a stick or board with a peg on the end which fits on the butt of the spear. It is like an extra length of arm, and makes the throw more powerful.

Hunters also used axes, clubs and various kinds of throwing stick. One kind, the boomerang which returns to the thrower, is famous, although not much used for hunting. It was used mainly for games.

Ways of hunting

There were two main ways of hunting. In one, many men worked together to surround the animals, or drive them towards other hunters who lay in ambush. The other more common way was for one man, or perhaps two, to stalk an animal.

Aborigines' tracking skills are famous. Hunters used disguises to get close to their prey. A man might hold a branch in front of him, or smear himself with earth, which stopped the animal getting his scent.

Patience

Hunters must have great patience, and even in the intense heat of the desert areas they may have to remain motionless for long periods, waiting for their prey.

It was important to know the ways of each creature. Emus, for instance, are inquisitive. One way of catching them was for a hunter to lie on his back and wave his legs in the air. The emu usually came to investigate.

A hunter divided a large animal among the other hunters and his relations in the camp. So no one went hungry and there was no waste.

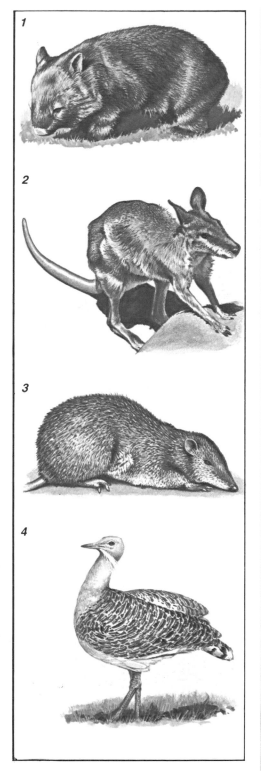

Left A man from Arnhem Land tests his spear in the early morning, to see if it has been warped by dew in the night. He is holding it in a spear-thrower. The stone head is covered with paper bark for protection.

Below Boyun and his catch of magpie geese.

Above A few of the animals which the Aborigines hunted for food.
1 The naked-nosed wombat is a badger-like creature. Aborigines smoked them out of holes in the ground
2 Hunters stalked agile wallabies, or drove them into nets.
3 People caught small animals like this Long-nosed bandicoot, often with the aid of dogs.
4 Larger birds like the great bustard were an important source of food.

Food from the waters

"They take that long-nosed canoe, and paddle along through the water . . .
With arms flexed, paddling. The wet paddle gleams in the sun."
Arnhem Land song

Fishing was very important to the people living on the coasts and rivers. Men speared fish or caught them with nets. Often they used boats to chase fish out over the water. They also caught turtles and seals, and occasionally killed whales stranded on the beaches.

Women stayed in shallow water, collecting shellfish. In some places they fished with lines and took part in fish drives. They made grass dams and pushed them through shallow water, so that the fish were forced to the water's edge and could be easily caught.

Poisonous plants

In rivers and inland pools other methods were used. Cleverly-made traps were laid, or poisonous plants, like native tobacco, were shredded into pools to stun the fish. They rose to the surface and could be collected.

The poison did not harm the people who ate the fish.

Boats and rafts

In the north-west, Aborigines made rafts out of logs. In the north they had learned from the Indonesians how to make dug-out canoes from tree trunks. But the most common kind of boat was the bark canoe.

This was made by stripping one large sheet of bark from a tree, binding the ends together and sealing them. A bark canoe could not make long voyages, but it worked well in rivers or near the coast. Such canoes were used a great deal on the Murray and Darling rivers.

Today, most Aborigines have gone from that area, and none live the old life any more there. However, you can see old trees, standing among modern houses, with the mark where the bark was taken from them.

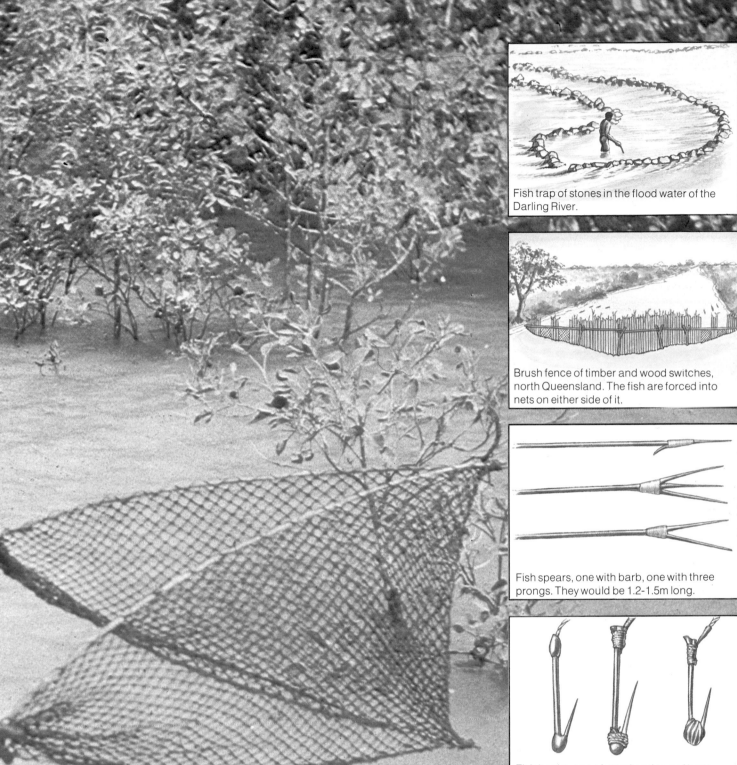

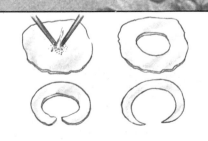

Fish trap of stones in the flood water of the Darling River.

Brush fence of timber and wood switches, north Queensland. The fish are forced into nets on either side of it.

Fish spears, one with barb, one with three prongs. They would be 1.2-1.5m long.

Fish hooks, one of wood and two of bone. Two pieces are stuck together with resin.

Making a fish hook of pearl shell. Burning makes the shell brittle, then it is ground into a crescent shape with a piece of coral.

A man fishing with a hand-net in a New South Wales river. When he has finished he will throw away the two sticks, and keep only the net: next time he will find two new sticks.

Fish and shellfish are still important in the diet of people who live on the coasts or by rivers.

Tools and trade

Below left Here you can see how clever Aborigines were at making one tool do several different jobs. These are only four of the ways a boomerang, could be used : there were many others.

Below Four stages in making a spear, in central Australia.

Aborigines had few possessions, for too many goods are a nuisance to people who move about, carrying everything themselves.

This was particularly true of desert-dwellers, who moved most often. They had the minimum of tools, but each could be used for many different purposes.

When people in the desert wanted to move, a man picked up his spear and thrower, a woman her dish and digging stick and they were ready.

Dress and decoration

Over most of the continent, people had almost no clothing, and did not need any. However, in the south, where it is cooler, they had fur cloaks made of the skin of possums, or other animals, sewn together. Sometimes the insides were painted.

Belts and necklaces were worn in many areas for decoration, or to show something about the wearer. For instance, a girl in Arnhem Land would wear a sort of harness round her breasts and shoulders, to show she was ready for marriage.

Exchanging gifts

Each person knew how to make almost everything he or she needed. But some things could only be found in certain places, or were made better there: for instance, the stones women used for grinding grain. Such things were obtained by trade.

There were no special traders. People exchanged things as gifts. For example, a man gave a hank of human-hair string to his friend and trading partner in the north, and received a pearl-shell ornament in return. After wearing this for a time, he exchanged it with a friend in the south for a carved boomerang, and so on, up and down the country.

A woman scrapes hot ashes over an animal in an earth oven.

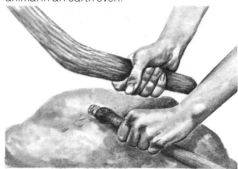
Here the boomerang is used to trim a stone-bladed adze.

Occasionally the boomerang took the place of a fire-saw.

The boomerang is used as a spade to dig a pit (to make an earth oven).

The spearmaker digs up a long root of an ironwood tree.

He strips off the outer bark with his teeth.

He trims it with a stone flake set in gum on the end of his spear-thrower.

He softens the spear shaft over a fire and makes sure it is straight.

Left This is how a spear-thrower (woomera) is used.

Below Australia was covered by a network of exchange routes. This map shows the main ones, with a few of the things that passed along them. **1** Finely worked Kimberley stone spear-point. **2** Pendant of pearl-shell, found off the northern coasts. **3** Carved boomerangs, being used to beat time. **4** Red ochre (iron oxide) for body paint. **5** *Pituri* (native tobacco). **6** Stone for axe-heads came from certain quarries.

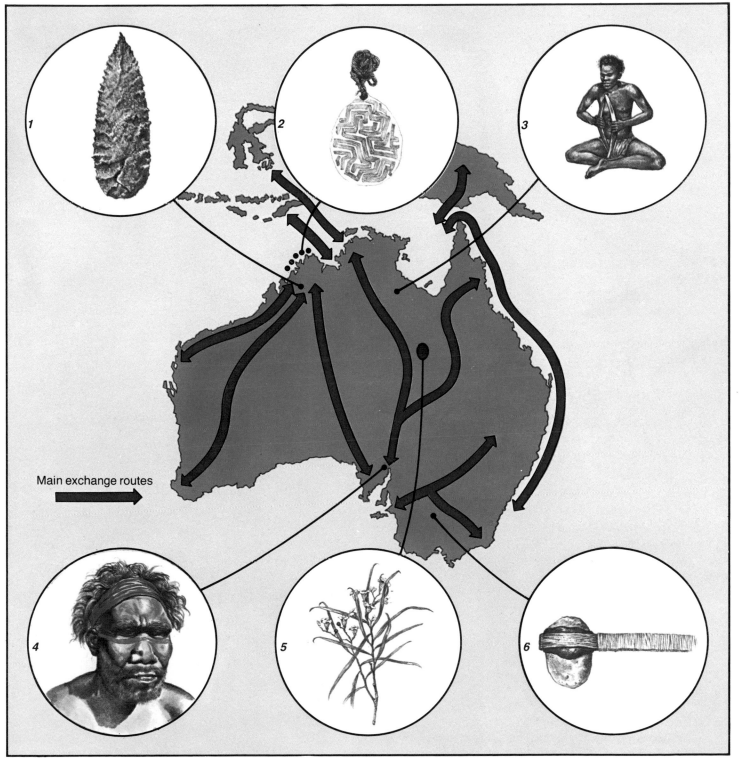

Main exchange routes

19

The Dreaming

Aborigines found the world full of everything they needed because, they believed, the Ancestors had made it so.

Long ago, there was just a flat emptiness. Then those great Beings came from under the earth, to make the hills and valleys, rivers and springs, animals and plants. Finally, they made human beings.

Generally the Ancestors had human forms, but they could take the shapes of animals and other things.

The Dreaming

There are many names for the time of the Ancestors. Some of these names also mean "dream", and Aborigines today, when they speak English, call that time "the Dreaming".

Few Aborigines nowadays get their living in the old way, but many still keep to their old religion. They have many different beliefs in different parts of the country, but all have to do with the Dreaming.

After the Ancestors had finished their work, they sank back into the earth. But they are still alive in the Dreaming, for that goes on for ever, though the creation period is past. Their bodies remain, as rocks or trees, still full of life-giving power.

Sacred places

Every clan has its sacred places. For example, Uluru, which white people call Ayers Rock, stands between the countries of two clans of the Pitjajantjara people: the Mala (a wallaby) and the Kunia (carpet snakes).

There the Ancestors of the clans (who also had the shapes of those animals) hunted, had children and performed ceremonies, setting the pattern of life for the people to follow. And the Rock still shows the signs of their deeds.

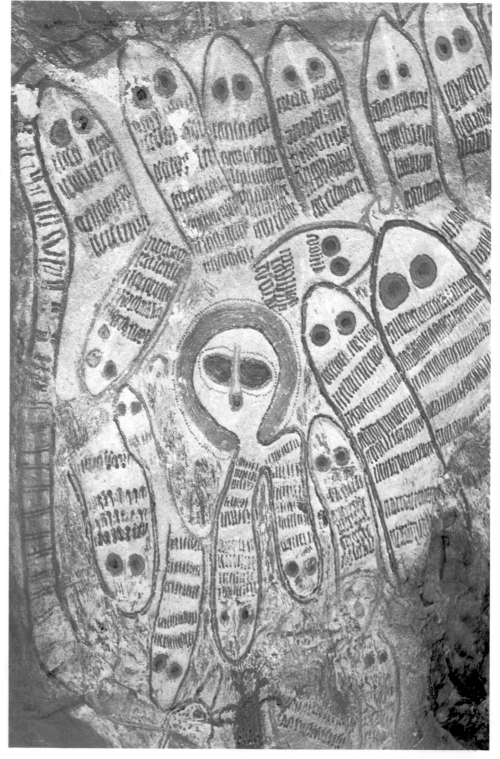

On the south side occurred the feud between the Kunia and the Liru. The woman Kunia Ingridi avenged the death of her son by killing a Liru: his brother in turn killed her daughter Tjinderi-Tjinderiba (Willy-Wagtail). Here too is the camp of Meta Lungana who was killed for being too mean to share his food. To the north is where the Mala were attacked by the demon-dog Kulpunia, during their initiation rites.

Camp where the Mala women waited while the young men were initiated. Kulpunia attacked and killed them.

Places where Kulpunia the demon-dog, stopped. He was sent by the enemies of the Mala to destroy them.

Camp of Tjinderi-Tjinderiba and her children. The rocks that were their bodies give life to babies.

Place where the young Mala men were being initiated when Kulpunia attacked them. They escaped, taking their sacred objects with them. The spot, which became a cave, was used for secret ceremonies ever after.

Where the Mala women gathered food. Piles of fruit they collected are now rocks. The life of the Ancestors was in many ways like that of the Aborigines later.

Camp of Meta Lungana, the sleepy-lizard man. He lived alone, and broke one of the most important laws by refusing to share the food he caught with others. Finally the Kunia men were so angry they killed him.

Where the Kunia woman Ingridi avenged her son by killing the chief Liru (poisonous snake) man. She cut off his nose with her digging stick; the nose is now a split-off piece of the rock, high up on the cliff.

Where the young Kunia man, Ingridi's son, died after he had been speared by the Liru warrior. The Liru came from the south and attacked the Kunia who were living there.

When Kunia Ingridi had lost her son and many of her other relations, killed by the Liru, she killed herself and her husband by chanting a magical song. These boulders were their bodies.

21

An ordered world

For the Mala clan, Mala wallabies are, in a way, kinsmen, since they too come from the Mala Ancestors. Clans are usually called after some animal, plant or thing, because the clan's Ancestors took its shape, or were connected with it in some way.

This animal, or plant or object, is something like a badge, as St. Patrick's shamrock is for the Irish. But it is more: there is supposed to be real kinship between it and the clan. For human beings and all other things have the same life in them, which comes from the Ancestors.

This kind of "badge" (some groups have several) is often called a "totem". But this word was not used by the Aborigines.

People divided
In many areas you would find the people divided into two "sides" which are generally called "moieties" in English. Each clan belongs to one or the other, and a person has to marry someone from the opposite moiety. For instance, Mala men generally marry Kunia girls.

Many groups have even more complicated rules about who may marry whom. This is bewildering to outsiders, but important to Aborigines who live in the traditional way. They are shocked by the way white people marry "just anybody".

The world divided
Since there are two sorts of people, and people and the world were organized by the Ancestors in the same way when the world was made, there must be two sorts of everything. So the north wind might belong to one moiety and the south wind to another; or the red kangaroo to one and the grey kangaroo to the other. Everything had its place.

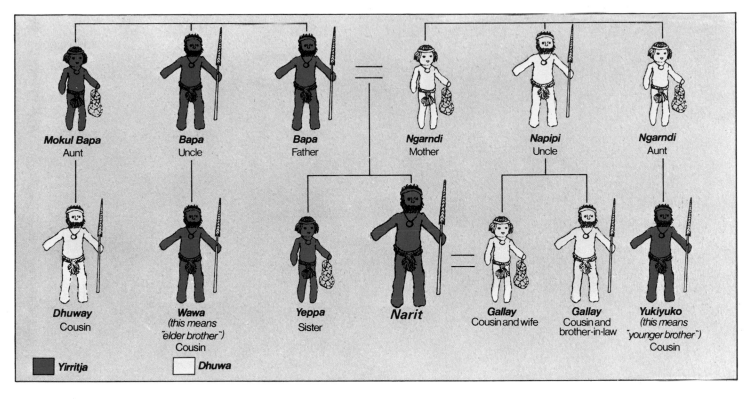

Mokul Bapa Aunt   **Bapa** Uncle   **Bapa** Father   **Ngarndi** Mother   **Napipi** Uncle   **Ngarndi** Aunt

Dhuway Cousin   **Wawa** *(this means "elder brother")* Cousin   **Yeppa** Sister   **Narit**   **Gallay** Cousin and wife   **Gallay** Cousin and brother-in-law   **Yukiyuko** *(this means "younger brother")* Cousin

■ **Yirritja**   □ **Dhuwa**

Above Traditionally, everyone an Aboriginal knew was a relation of some kind. Their terms for kin are therefore different from ours, and much more complicated. Words that we translate as "brother" or "aunt" may actually cover scores of people for an Aboriginal.

This diagram shows how the moieties work in north-east Arnhem Land where they are called *Dhuwa* and *Yirritja*.

People here belong to their father's clan and moiety. In some places they would belong to their mother's. The central character is a man, Narit. The other words are all kinship terms.

The sign = stands for marriage. Narit is *Yirritja* like his father. His mother is *Dhuwa* and so is the cousin whom he marries. His father could also be married to his aunt on the mother's side, but does not have to be.

Left These wood carvings from Arnhem Land show ancestral heroes. They too are either *Dhuwa (left)* or *Yirritja (right)*.

Right In north-east Arnhem Land, each clan has sacred designs which are used on sacred objects and on the bodies of clan members, in ceremonies. The designs refer to the clan's Ancestors, and the country they made. The design on the left comes from a *Dhuwa* clan, that on the right is *Yirritja*.

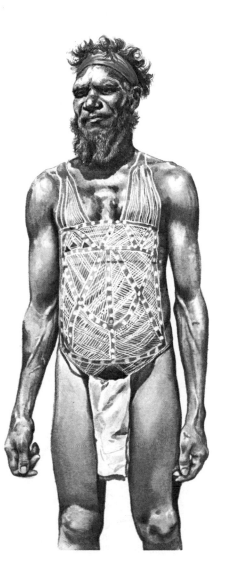 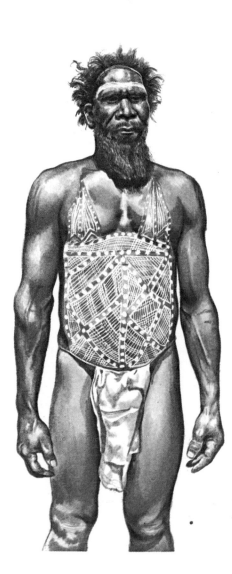

23

Song and ceremony

"I call the didgeridu man here . . .
How we danced when those two girls came down!"
Arnhem Land song

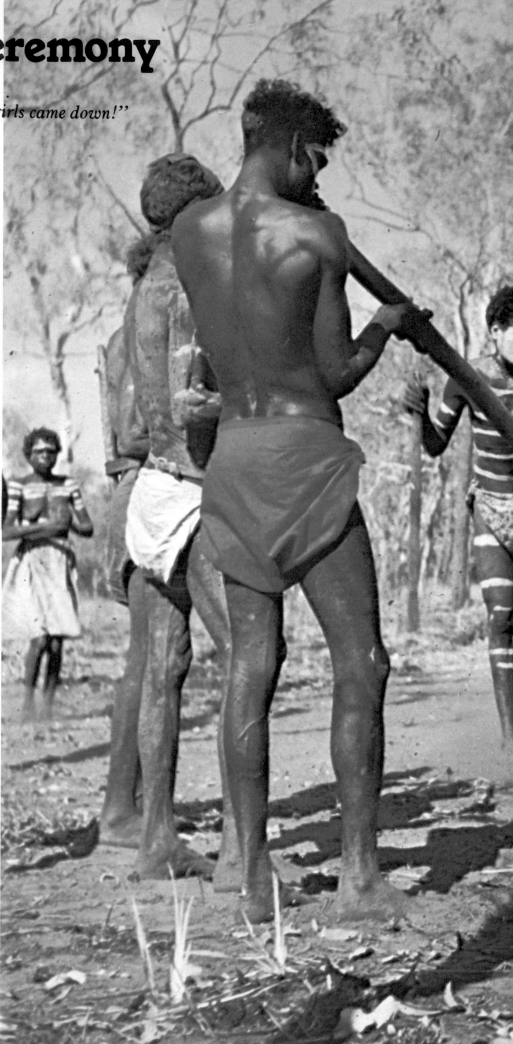

To amuse themselves, people had ball games and many other sports. In the evenings a favourite pastime was, and still is, dancing and singing. Some dances imitate the movements of animals, or tell a story. People often decorate themselves for their parts in these stories.

Sacred rites
The more elaborate dances form ceremonies which have religious meaning. Many people gather for an important ceremony, which may last for days.

However, the greatest and most sacred ceremonies are the secret rites which only fully adult men may see. Through these rites the men summon the power of the Ancestors, so that plants and animals and people will grow, and life will keep on its proper course. Women too have their rites, which are secret from men.

Kinds of song
Singing usually goes with dancing. Anyone may make up a song, though some people are especially good at it, and may grow famous.

Some songs are about everyday life, like the one translated above. Sacred songs are inspired by the Ancestors through the dreams of older men.

Here is part of a long set of such songs, from the Mudbara people of the desert. They are sung in chorus: each line is one song, and is repeated over and over again.

"Day breaks, the first rays of the rising sun, stretching her arms.
Day breaks, as the sun rises to her feet.
Sun rising, scattering the darkness, lighting the land . . .
With disc shining, bringing daylight, as birds whistle and call . . ."

24

The 'Rom' ceremony, shown here taking place in Arnhem Land, can be either for trading or ceremonial exchange between different tribes. It also signifies friendship between the tribes. A man accompanies the dancers on the *didgeridoo*. This is a long wooden pipe with a droning note, typical of north Australia.

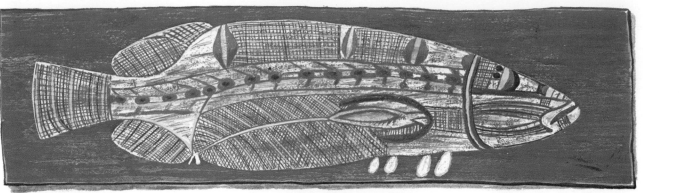

One of the things people have always liked to do round the fire in the evenings is to tell stories.

Some stories are made up on the spot, but there are hundreds that have been handed down from the past. Some of these are tales or legends from the Dreaming, but others may be about things that have happened to the story-teller's grandparents, or uncles or other relatives.

The famous paintings on bark, from Arnhem Land, often show scenes from legends.

Left A scene from the sacred story of the Wawalag sisters, two important Ancestors of Arnhem Land. The snakes from the water hole all over the country stand up to ask the greatest among them, Witit, what he has done with the two women.
Bottom left *Mimi,* kindly spirits of western Arnhem Land legend, among some animals.
Centre bottom The woman Adurimja brings water-lily bulbs for her children to eat.
Far right The Morning Stars in the Land of the Dead. The old woman is in the centre, with two stars on each side. Around her are the yams which the ghosts eat.
Top right Aborigines used to record interesting events (like the arrival of these doctors) in their rock paintings. Now this is often done on bark.

How the tortoise got his shell
Echidna is an animal like a hedgehog. But in the Dreaming she was a woman, and Tortoise was a man. One day they quarrelled over a snail they both wanted to eat. At last Tortoise grew so angry he picked up a bundle of bamboo-spears and threw them at Echidna: they stuck in her back and became spikes. So she picked up a large flat stone and threw it at Tortoise. It stuck on his back and became a shell. And that is how they became what they are today.

The Morning Stars
Once a man called Yalngura saw a yam leaf blown towards him on the wind. He knew that the wind was blowing from Bralgu, across the sea, where the spirits of *Yirritja* people go after death. The idea came to him to sail there. He said goodbye to his wives and children and set out.

He had with him a sacred spear-thrower fringed with human hair, of the kind the ghosts use, so that they would take him for a friend.

After paddling for several days, Yalngura reached Bralgu. The ghosts made him welcome. They gave him yams to eat, and three girls to be his wives.

Then they showed him the Morning Stars, which are kept in a

basket by an old woman. At first she did not want to show Yalngura the stars, but he sang a magic song, and finally she brought them out.

He saw that they were feathered balls on long strings, just like the ones they used at his home, in the Morning Star ceremonies for the dead. But these were alive and could fly.

Yalngura sang the Morning Star songs:

"Banambir, Morning Star . . .
Rising, rising, attached to its string
Above Wuguludjedju, Baleibalei.

Following the water, following the
water all the way,
Feathered ball on its string, rising,
Shining brightly at Wuluti,
Coming from Bralgu.

Ghosts, lifting their arms as they
dance . . .
Dancing along, with hooked fingernails
Dancing there in the darkness, in pitch
darkness, at Bralgu,
At Wuguludjangalu . . . at
Baleibalei . . ."

As Yalngura sang, the old woman sent out the stars to all the places he had named. Then, as the day began to break, she pulled them in by their strings and put them in her basket.

Yalngura made ready to return home. The other ghosts loaded his canoe with gifts; but his three wives stood on the beach and cried to see him go.

At last he reached the shores of his home. His family were joyful and they feasted on the yams and other good things he had brought back.

Afterwards they all lay down to sleep. But in the morning Yalngura was dead. His ghost wives wanted him back, and had taken his soul.

A *Mamu* story
Children in the western desert are terrified by the stories about *Mamu*. These are terrible creatures with long bloody teeth and nails like claws, who catch unwary travellers and carry them off to their homes underground, which are strewn with human bones. They can also turn themselves into shapes of other things.

Once a hunter, carrying home the animal he had killed, saw a sharp flake of stone lying on the ground. He picked it up thinking it was just what he needed to sharpen his spear.

He sat down and lit a fire to cook the meat. Meanwhile he got out the flake and the spear. But the sharp stone jumped out of his hand and cut his throat.

The stone was a *Mamu* woman and she was the one who had the dinner.

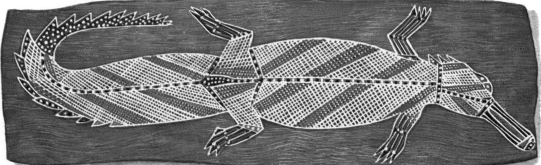

Childhood

"In its own Wungar place   She appeared to me . . .
A spirit waits for birth . . .   I understood suddenly
As I looked at the water   The life in our baby –
of Bundaalunaa   Her name is Dragon Fly."
Kimberley Elder, Sam Woolagoodjah (translated)

Aborigines believe the Ancestors left certain places full of the life which makes new children. The rock beside Uluru, which was once the body of Tjinderi-Tjinderiba, is one such place.

The Pitjajantjara say that spirits waiting to be born look like tiny versions of small children. Sometimes people catch a glimpse of them standing around their camp fire, but if you go near, they vanish.

Special ties

When a woman goes near one of those places, a spirit may enter her body to be born later as a baby. She knows this has happened when she feels the baby moving in her stomach for the first time. All its life the child will have a special tie with that place.

In northern Arnhem Land they say that the spirit appears in the shape of an animal to the man who will be its father, when he is hunting. When the child is born, it is believed he will have a kinship with that animal.

Initiation

Children stay mostly with their mothers, learning bit by bit the skills they will need in adult life.

For a girl, growing up is mostly a gradual thing, but for a boy the end of childhood comes suddenly. In his mid-teens or earlier he is taken away from his mother and brought to a special camp with the other boys.

Adult men form a kind of secret society and if boys are to grow up they must be initiated into it.

The boys may go through loneliness and pain, being circumcised or having a tooth knocked out, before they can go home as men. And they know they must never tell the younger boys or the women what they have seen and heard.

Above A boy from north-east Arnhem Land. He is being decorated and people are singing over him, in preparation for his circumcision ceremony. Boys in this area may be initiated from the age of seven.

Left Pannyi, a girl from Western Australia, collecting quandongs. Their juicy outer coats are a good source of food. Boys and girls learn quickly by copying the grown-ups.

Below Pannyi with her dogs.

28

Below Children from Mornington Island playing with a turtle. Sea turtles are eaten, along with dugong, and fish such as mullet, salmon and barramundi.

Later life

After a boy's initiation there is more to learn and other stages to go through before he is fully a man. Then he can play his part in the religious rites which keep human and animal life going. He can marry, too, generally at about 25.

Both men and women have their own secret ceremonies in many parts of the continent. While the men's ceremonies are about questions of life and death, those of the women are to do with keeping everyone in good health.

Marriage

Marriage in the old way of life had little to do with romance. It was a practical business. A man, or his family, would look for a suitable girl, belonging to the group he ought to marry into. It was an arrangement between the families, not just between two people. The couple were not expected to be "in love", though they might well grow to love each other as time went on.

Arrangements for marriage are simple. As soon as she is old enough, the girl and her husband start camping together, usually with no special ceremony. Often they spend the first years living with the wife's family. The husband has to give his wife's parents presents of food and other things.

Runaway couples

People always fell in love of course, and sometimes couples who were not supposed to marry ran off together. If they wanted to come back their marriage was generally accepted in the end.

Men might have more than one wife. In some places, important older men had six or more. But most had only one at a time.

Below An Arnhem Land family set out on a food-gathering expedition.

30

Right People mourning a relative's death have to keep strict rules during their period of mourning. This Tiwi man from Melville Island is a chief mourner: he may not handle food, so his wife feeds him.

Elders

As a man grew older he learned more about life and its religious secrets.

This is still true for those who live in Northern Australia. Old men are expected to be wise, and younger men should obey them. It is the business of the Elders to organize the great rites, and pass on traditions.

Death and afterwards

When a person dies, his or her relatives mourn with loud wailing, often wounding themselves with knives and clubs. There used to be various ways of disposing of the body, though not all are practised now. It could be buried, or burnt, or placed on a platform of branches and left.

Often, in Arnhem Land, the family collect the bones and keep them. It may be months or years before they finally say goodbye to what is left of their relative.

All this time, they believe, the person's spirit is nearby. Only when the last funeral ceremonies are over will it finally leave.

Most Aborigines believe that some part of a person will survive. It will go back to the place in the earth that it came from, or as they say in northern Arnhem Land, to the Land of the Dead across the sea.

Left A funeral procession on the lower Murray river in 1864. The corpse is carried in a bark canoe, and the mourners follow.

Right A hollow log bone coffin with goanna totem designs holds this man's relative's bones.

Peace, feud and revenge

In the old life, there was nothing that people nowadays would call government. There were no kings or chiefs, and no police.

People sometimes wonder how, without these things, people can live together in peace and order.

Part of the answer is that people fear what the others in their group think of them. To be hated or made fun of by the people you live with is a worse punishment than any threat of prison. This sort of ridicule was usually enough to settle small offences, but for more serious crimes Aborigines had strict rules laid down for dealing with offenders.

Throwing spears

People did sometimes wrong each other. There was very little stealing: there was no point, since the few things a person needed were easy to make. But people quarrelled and hurt each other, or trespassed on forbidden sacred places, or on hunting grounds they were not supposed to use.

Men were expected to punish their own wives and families if they misbehaved. Brothers could discipline their sisters. Older men tried to settle quarrels between families.

Sometimes two men with a dispute would fight a duel with spears. Or the culprit would have to stand still while the offended man threw spears at him until he was wounded.

Feuding

A quarrel between people of different clans might lead to serious blood-feuds. Raiding parties attacked the camp of the other side. Many people were killed in such raids.

One way to try to end a feud was to challenge the other side to a formal battle, to settle all scores.

Sorcery

As well as fighting with clubs and spears there was another way of killing people: by sorcery. If anyone died of disease, especially if he or she was not really old, people believed it must be the fault of some jealous person practising magic. There were various magical tests to find out who was responsible.

The injured person, or a relative of the dead person, would then try to take revenge, either by attacking the camp of the killer, or more probably by using sorcery on him.

Killing or curing

Certain Elders, people believed, had special skills of killing by magic. Such a man would creep up on his victim, kill him, and take out the fat or another part of his insides.

Then he would close the wound, bring the person back to life, and make him go home as usual. But a day or two later, the far-away sorcerer would burn the fat, and the person would drop dead.

This was just one of many ways of causing death or illness. But anybody skilled in magic could cure a sick person too. Almost anyone could practise the simple kinds of magic, but "making a person alive to die" could only be done by those with special training.

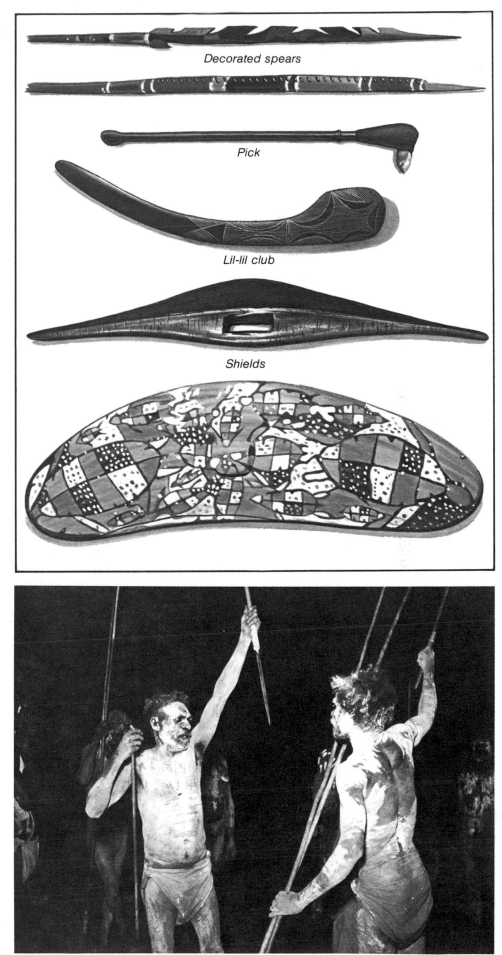

Decorated spears

Pick

Lil-lil club

Shields

The white invasion

"White man got no Dreaming,
Him go 'nother way.
White man, him go different,
Him go road bilong himself."
Unknown 19th-century Aborigine

In 1770 Captain James Cook landed at Cape York and claimed Australia for the British Empire. From then on the lives of Aborigines were changed by things that were happening on the other side of the world.

The first use the British made of their new territory was to start penal colonies in it, to ease the overcrowding in English prisons.

Wealth from the land

It was not until the nineteenth century that settlers really started to open up the country. In Britain factories were being built, cities were growing, there were more people than ever before. The land of Australia could produce things that people at home wanted.

Farmers found that much of Australia's land was ideal for grazing sheep. The wool was shipped back to be made into cloth in the new factories. Later settlers started to raise cattle, and grow wheat and other crops to sell in Britain.

Another kind of wealth lay under the earth. Gold was discovered in New South Wales in the 1850s, and later in many other places.

Immigrants

Australia could also take more and more people from Britain. These immigrants started colonies in different parts of the continent. Later, with independence from Britain, these colonies became States, each one with its own Parliament.

In 1901 they were joined into the Commonwealth of Australia but the federal government could not make laws about Aborigines in the different States until 1967.

The dream of the immigrants was of a fresh start in an empty land. Only it was not empty.

Left The gold rushes brought people from all over the world to seek their fortunes. This is Mount Alexander, in the 1850s.

Right John Batman buys the land where Melbourne now stands for a price which includes 10 looking-glasses and 50 handkerchiefs. This was the only time Aborigines were paid anything at all for their land, but the Crown annulled the treaty.

Below In this early 19th-century picture, a sailor is threatened while collecting firewood.

Above Europeans were not the first foreigners to land in Australia. For a century or more, fishermen from Indonesia had been visiting the Arnhem Land coast in boats like this, a Malay prau, shown here on a bark painting.

Right This rock painting of a horse is on Cape York, Queensland. The first horses were brought to that area during the gold rush of the 1870s, when Europeans arrived in large numbers. Aborigines showed new experiences such as this in their paintings, as they always had done.

Losing the land

"There used to be a lot of people here: kids splashing in the water, laughing, singing – but now they are all gone, nothing left now."

An old man who had lost his land

The Aborigines believed that the Ancestors had given them their land, to look after and keep. Many of the white newcomers believed God had given them the land as a sort of construction kit, to be made into something else.

To people who think like this, as many still do, anyone who does not change, or "develop" the land has no right to be on it. A settler thought that if the local Aborigines hunted over the part he had marked out for himself, then *they* were trespassers.

The law of the new white Australia said that Aborigines had no right at all to the land.

Remnants

Bit by bit, the white settlers occupied the continent, and everywhere they came the Aborigines died. In the south and south-east only remnants of the groups who had lived there were left by the middle of the 19th century.

But in the far north and the desert centre, many Aboriginal groups stayed for a long time undisturbed. In parts of the desert there were people who had never seen a white man until the 1960s.

Bullets and disease

By 1900 the number of Aborigines had dropped from about 300,000 to about 66,000. Many had died from bullets and many more from diseases, such as tuberculosis, which they caught from the whites.

The rest had lost their land and their sacred places, the homes of their souls. It was not their world any longer and nothing made any sense. The Aborigines became despondent, and the death rate rose dramatically. Soon, it seemed, there would be no more Aborigines.

Above Queensland 1886: Native troopers dispersing a camp. The Queensland Native Police were Aborigines recruited into the Government service. "Dispersing" became a polite way of saying "killing".

Left When the wild game they had lived on was driven away, the Aborigines speared settlers' cattle for food. They also did it as an act of war, hoping to drive the white people out. Here the owner of the cattle arrives and shoots the Aborigines.

Left Aborigines were often friendly and helpful to white people. These two acted as guides to the explorer Ludwig Leichhardt in the 1840s. Along with their clothes they were given new names: Charley and Harry Brown.

Right Many Aboriginal groups died out altogether from bullets, disease and ill-treatment. The best known of those who died were the Tasmanians. When the white people arrived, there were probably about 4,000. By 1847 there were only 47 left. Here are nine at Oyster Cove.

The quotations below show what life could be like for Aborigines. The first is from a man in Queensland in 1904:

"Then the white men came among us, we were hunted from our ground, shot, poisoned, and had our daughters, sisters and wives taken from us . . . They stole our ground where we used to get food, and when we got hungry and took a bit of flour or killed a bullock to eat, they shot us or poisoned us. All they give us now for our land is a blanket once a year".

The second is the memory of an old man in Kimberley, of what happened when he was a small boy in the 1880s. His people had killed a white man, and they had been raided and killed in return. He and his sister were found hiding behind a tree by a party of white people:

" 'Better shoot 'em', one of the white men said. 'This little boy only gonna grow up to put a spear in some poor white fella, and this little girl, well she gonna breed more blackfellers.'

Then big Duncan McCaully come up. 'I can do with a boy' he says, and he puts me up on his saddle, and somebody else took Maggie . . ."

To shoot Aborigines like that was against the law. But in the vast frontier areas, neither settlers nor police always bothered about that.

Right The surviving Tasmanians were rounded up from their territory and put in a special settlement. They were homesick there, and more and more died. The last man died in 1865. The last full-blooded Tasmanian of all was Truganini, shown here in her old age. She died in 1876, begging that her body would not be given to scientists for examination, as others had been. *Don't let them cut me up, bury me behind the mountains."* Nevertheless, her bones were kept in a museum case until 1976. Then, in a special ceremony, her body was cremated.

A changed world

"No more boomerang
No more spear;
Now all civilized –
Colour bar and beer.
Kath Walker

No more sharing
What the hunter brings.
Now we work for money
Then pay it back for things."

Below Yuendumu reserve, Northern Territory, 1978. In the old life, people moved camp and left their waste behind, where it soon rotted into the earth. In camps like these today, people have to live there all the time. Tin cans pile up and there is no sanitation.

Decent permanent housing is hard to get for people as poor as most Aborigines. When they move into towns they have the worst housing, or none at all. Many Aborigines live in camps similar to this, on the edge of towns.

For the surviving Aborigines, the question was how to live in this strange new world. But for the white people and their governments, the question was: what to do about the Aborigines?

At different times the white people tried two different answers.

One was to ignore Aborigines, in the belief that they were bound to die out anyway. Meanwhile, they could be given handouts of food. Also, areas of land were set aside as reserves for them to live in. But even these did not belong by law to Aborigines, but to the State.

Not wanted

The other answer was that Aborigines should give up everything to do with their old way of life, learn to take jobs, and become just like white Australians.

More and more Aborigines tried to do this. But all too often they found they were not wanted. They could get no jobs, or only the most menial and worst paid. They were not allowed to live in the towns, only in camps on the fringes. If children went to school, teachers rarely bothered with them.

Wrong

Besides this, to "succeed" in the white man's world meant learning new ways of behaving. Some of these were only strange and unfamiliar, but others went quite against Aborigines' ideas of right and wrong.

For instance, it was the duty of a man to share all he brought home with his relations. But this meant that if he had a job and they had not, he could never save any money.

So those Aborigines who lost their land were forced to be dependent on any casual work offered them, or on handouts from the government.

Left Up to World War II, this old man, Paddy, who was an elder among his people, received only his food, two suits of clothes a year, and the title "King" for his work as a stockman on a cattle station, but no wages. The law (not always obeyed) has now made wages for Aborigines and white people equal.

Below This woman at Elliot Clinic carries her baby in a wooden "coolamon". The number of Aboriginal babies who die is high, though less than ten years ago. The Aboriginal birth rate is twice that of white Australians.

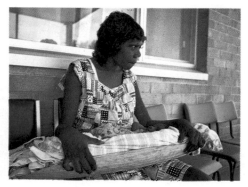

38

Above Humpty Doo Camp near Darwin, Northern Territory.

Left Daly River Mission School. Missionaries have founded villages for Aborigines to settle in. Although they have been blamed for destroying Aboriginal traditions, missionaries have shown concern for Aborigines when few other white people did. At another mission (*below left*) women make mats for sale.

Below A carpentry workshop.

The poor Australians

"We are the drifters, the faceless ones.
Turn your heads as we walk by
We are the lost, forgotten sons
Bereft in a land of plenty."
Jack Davis, Aboriginal poet and leader

Today there are at least 150,000 people of Aboriginal descent.

Among them are successful business people, artists, writers and entertainers, sportsmen and sportswomen, and three elected politicians. But these are exceptions. Most of the other people are just very poor.

In 1976 more than half of all Aborigines were unemployed. In the country areas only two men in every ten had a job.

Disease and death

Poverty means homelessness, or bad housing, not enough food, or the wrong kind of food. In 1977 doctors estimated that 25 per cent of the Aboriginal babies in a poor area of Sydney were undernourished.

As many babies die in their first year among the Aborigines as in the world's poorest countries. In the Northern Territory in 1972, 87 died out of every thousand born, compared with only 17 in every thousand white Australian babies. Those who live often suffer from diseases which damage their sight and hearing.

Making decisions

Coming from this background, children find things difficult at school. Most drop out in their early teens, so do not have much prospect of a better life.

Like underprivileged minorities in every country, many Aborigines escape from their troubles in alcohol.

More and more Aborigines are now fighting to change these conditions. They are claiming, too, the right to take decisions for themselves instead of always taking orders from white people. And they are making their voices heard.

Below The main Aboriginal reserves today. The former reserves in the Northern Territory are now Aboriginal Land. The dots show other Aboriginal communities. There are also Aborigines in most towns and cities.

In the north and centre of the continent, the majority are still anxious to live in a way related to the past.

In the south and east most people live in towns and speak only English, their traditional life is only a memory.

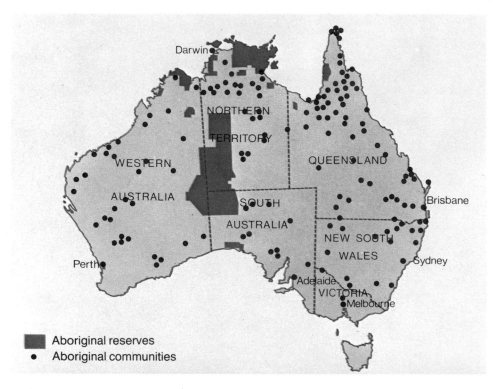

- ■ Aboriginal reserves
- • Aboriginal communities

Above Dennis Walker, active in politics.

Left Galarrwuy Yunupingu. He is Chairman of the Northern Land Council, which manages Aboriginal Lands in the northern part of the Northern Territory. He takes part in both traditional life and modern politics.

Right In 1972 this tent "Embassy" was put up in front of Government House, Canberra. It lasted six months, and news about Aboriginal affairs (particularly about land rights) was broadcast from it all over Australia.

Above Kath Walker, born in Queensland, is a writer, and works for Aboriginal rights.

Left Evonne Goolagong, the tennis star. She wrote in her life story, *"Now we Aborigines are aliens in our own land . . . we are looked down on for the most part. I might be looked down on too except that I can do something that is . . . respected in this civilization by its white majority."*

Below Gulpilil, the actor. He appeared in the films *Storm Boy* and *Walkabout*.

The way ahead

"We Aborigines, we like to live the quiet way. We like to go hunting, to sleep in the bush and listen to the birds singing, the animals crying, stomping their feet on the salt plains . . . now we don't have those things. There's the noise of bulldozers and cars and aeroplanes."
Mrs. Joyce Hall, North Queensland Land Council

Aborigines today want better schools for their children; the right to settle their own quarrels by their own traditional laws; and above all the right to own the lands which were once theirs alone.

Aborigines who are still close to the traditional life live in the large reserves of the north and centre of Australia. They were left in peace there because nobody else wanted that land.

Now minerals have been found there which are wanted by modern industries: iron, aluminium and uranium. Mining for these means stripping the whole countryside.

Land rights

Until recently, Aborigines in most parts of Australia did not own their land, so they could simply be moved off it. In Queensland, where mining is going on, people have had to leave their homes and have been paid nothing.

So Aborigines all over Australia are joining in the fight for land rights, with some success. In 1978, Arnhem Land and the other reserves in the Northern Territory were declared by law to be "Aboriginal Land". In South Australia the North West Reserve (114,000 square kilometres) is to be put under Aboriginal control.

The way ahead

Aborigines want changes in education too. At one time there were ten times more white than Aboriginal children in upper forms of secondary schools.

Now there are grants to help children stay on at school. The Aboriginal Arts Board also gives scholarships, so that gifted children can study at home or abroad. The way ahead looks much brighter now.

Above A demonstration against "white racism".

Left Mick Miller, Chairman of the North Queensland Land Council, and Mrs. Joyce Hall from Weipa, now taken over by a bauxite (aluminium) mine. They toured Europe in 1978 to explain their struggle for land rights.

Right Mount Tom Price in the Hamersley Range, Western Australia. Hamersley Iron's open-pit mine is a mountain of iron ore six kilometres long. It is to make way for such mining activities that Aborigines are turned off their land.

Things to do

Palm leaf basket, from Queensland

For your "palm leaf" use green or brown paper (sugar paper is ideal) cut out in an oval about 60mm by 40mm. It is folded like the end of a parcel. (1) Make a fold about a third of the way up. (2) and (3) fold the two ends across. (4) Gum them together. You can paint or draw in the stitches which would hold the palm leaf together.

In the original basket, the handle is made from the stalk of the leaf, as shown in the drawings. You will probably have to cut it from a separate strip of paper, in which case it will be easier to stick it on at the end.

You can make a more permanent basket from canvas or another fairly stiff material, sewing the ends and the handle together.

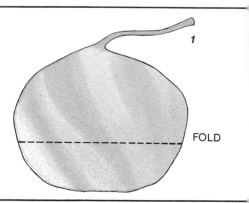

String or raffia bag

This is slightly adapted from one of the many Aboriginal techniques. Fairly thick string is easiest to work with. Make a loop of string, the size of the mouth of your bag, leaving a "tail" of extra string.
(1) Put it over a peg, the knob of a chair, or similar, and hold it taut with your left hand. (2) Take another length of string: knot one end on to the base string. Thread the end over and down as shown. Repeat until you have gone all the way round. Make the second row of loops into the first row. (3) At this point take the whole thing off the peg, and join on a fresh length of string as shown. Try to keep all the knots in a line. When the bag is long enough, sew up the bottom, and use base string as a handle.

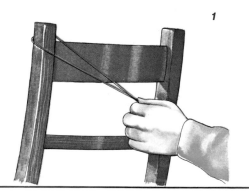

A cardboard boomerang

This works in the same way as a real returning boomerang.
(1) Cut a piece of stiff card in the shape shown. It can be anything from 76mm to 150mm long. (2) Bend up the tip a little along the line shown. (3) To fly the boomerang, put it on a support (such as this book) holding it down gently with your left thumb. The slight twist should be turned up towards you. Give the other end a good flick with your right finger so that it spins away from under your thumb. It will take some practice to get the flick right, so persevere. If it stops spinning too soon and falls down, check the end is not twisted too sharply. (4) You could also make a wooden boomerang. You can find instructions in *The Boomerang Book* by J. M. Hansen (Puffin).

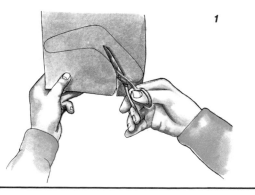

Card from a bark painting design

The artists of Arnhem Land use only four colours for their bark paintings: red and yellow (ochre), white (clay), and black (charcoal). You can copy their designs, or invent your own in the same style, using powder or poster paints on brown paper.

You can print a greetings card, using self-hardening clay.
(1) Flatten the clay on a smooth surface. Turn it smooth side up. Outline the design with a knitting needle. Smooth the edges around the groove, and leave to dry. (2) Lightly cover the shape with tempera paint or ink. (3) Place a piece of matt-surfaced paper on it and smooth down gently. (4) Carefully peel it off, cut out the design and mount it on card.

When you have all the prints you want, you can varnish the clay plaque.

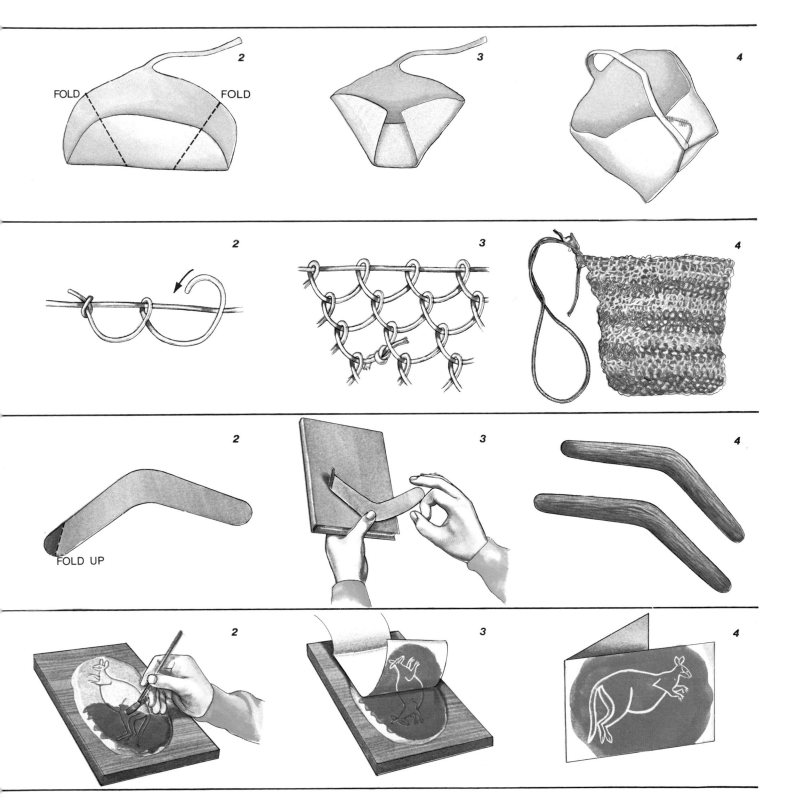

FOLD   FOLD   2

3

4

2

3

4

2

FOLD UP

3

4

2

3

4

Reference

Aboriginal languages

There were perhaps five hundred languages spoken in Australia when the first white men arrived, though many of them no longer exist. But they have some things in common which show they were once one language.

For example, none of them has the sound "s", except for the languages in the north of Queensland. They picked it up from New Guinea.

Few Aboriginal words have been taken into English, although people who shout "Coo-ee", in fact are using an Aboriginal call. Many Australian place names, however, are Aboriginal words. Canberra, the name of the Commonwealth capital, comes from a word meaning "meeting place".

Place names

Here are some names from New South Wales, some from vanished languages:

Balagong, "feeding ground of the kangaroo".
Gowrie, "down of the eaglehawk".
Beebari, "place of a large brown snake".
Wollumbi, "meeting of the waters".
Myuna, "clear water".
Marangaroo, "little blue flower".

Special languages

Some Europeans think that Aboriginal languages must be simple. In fact, they are as complicated as any other language and no easier or harder to learn. Most Aboriginal groups also have special languages, like codes, for certain people or times.

There may be a language of respect that a man uses to his mother-in-law and other senior women. Sometimes there is a secret language for older men, used in ceremonies.

Sometimes Aborigines are not allowed to talk: when they are being initiated for example, or when they are mourning the death of a relative. Then they use sign languages. The signs are also useful when you are out hunting and must be quiet.

Aborigines from different places with different languages can understand each other too.

Below are some signs from Queensland. (There are hundreds of others.) The sign for "child" really means "thinks the same".

When Aborigines first met Europeans they often learned "pidgin English" (see the poem on page 34). This is a mixed language that sounds funny to English-speaking people.

Because of this, some people have the wrong idea that Aborigines "can't talk properly". Aborigines only spoke like that because the early settlers taught them to do so.

Sources of information

Australia House, Aldwych, London, WC2 has a good reference library.
The Commonwealth Institute, Kensington High Street, London W8, lends tapes, books and filmstrips.
Pictorial Charts Education Trust, 27 Kirchen Road, London W13 3UD, has a set of wallcharts.
Survival International, 36 Craven Street, London WC2, gives information on Aborigines.
Aboriginal Publications Foundation, Shop 9, International House, 2 Irwin Street, Perth, Western Australia, publishes *Identity.*
Department of Aboriginal Affairs, Canberra, Australian Capital Territory, Australia.
Aboriginal Cultural Foundation, Smith Street, Darwin, N.T., Australia.

Films for hire

Scottish Central Film Library, 16 Woodside Terrace, Glasgow has a series of films on the traditional life of desert people.
I.D. Television Ltd., Craven Lodge, 15-17 Craven Hill, London W2 3ER, have a series on rock art and traditional life.
War on Want, 467 Caledonian Road, London N1, has films on present day problems.

Museums

Museum of Mankind, London.
Horniman Museum, London.
Manchester Museum.
Royal Scottish Museum, Edinburgh.
Art Galleries and Museum, Glasgow.

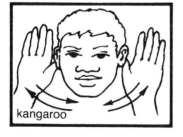

kangaroo

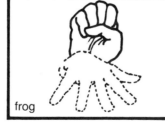

frog

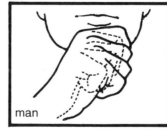

man

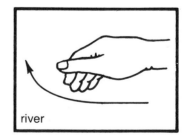

river

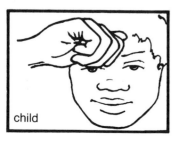

child

snake

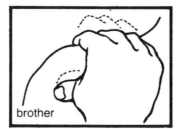

brother

duck

Glossary

Aborigines From the Latin *aborigine* meaning "from the beginning". It is a name used for people all over the world who were "there first", but specially for the native people of Australia.

Adze A kind of axe, with the cutting edge at right angles to the handle.

Boomerang A word from a language of a people who used to live in New South Wales (perhaps their word for wind). It means a throwing stick, used as a weapon in many parts of Australia. The famous returning boomerang was used mainly as a toy.

Clan A group of people who believe they are all descended from the same person: in this book used only for groups related in either the male or female line. The people of an Aboriginal clan are generally thought to come from one Ancestor. Together they own one or more stretches of country: the clan territory.

Coroboree A word from an Aboriginal language used to mean any sort of dance or ceremony.

Digeridoo A kind of trumpet played by Aborigines of the north and northeast, made of a hollow piece of wood or bamboo about a metre long.

Dreaming English name for the "sacred time" of the Ancestors, which once was, and eternally is. It is not at all the same as ordinary dreaming, though people may get in touch with it through dreams.

Initiation The ceremony of entering a group or society. The initiation of an Aboriginal boy makes him part of his clan's religious life.

Moiety A word for half, used when a tribe is divided in two.

Pituri A plant for chewing, but also used as a kind of tobacco.

Totem Any animal, plant or thing, with which people believe they have a special relationship. Totems are not worshipped.

Tribe In Australia, a group of neighbouring clans who speak the same language and know each other. One "tribe" may merge with another in time.

Woomera A spear-thrower.

Yam A plant whose root is an important food in most tropical countries.

Book list

Aborigines by Ben Burt (Museum of Mankind booklet) is a short factual account of traditional life.
Bush Walkabout by Axel Poignant (Angus and Robertson) is a photo story suitable for younger children.
The Aborigines by R. M. Gibbs (Longman) is for young readers.

For older readers:
The Dark Australians by Douglass Baglin and David Moore (Australia and N.Z. Book Co.). Also published by John Weatherhill as *"People of the Dreamtime"*.
The First Australians by R. M. and C. H. Berndt (Ure-Smith).
Triumph of the Nomads by Geoffrey Blainey (Macmillan Australia).

On the present day situation:
Living Black by Kevin Gilbert (Alan Lane). The writer is Aboriginal.
Australia's Policy Towards Aborigines by H. C. Coombs (Minority Rights Group).
From Massacres to Mining Companies by Jan Roberts (War on Want).

Stories for young readers include:
The Ice is Coming by Patricia Wrightson, Hutchinson: stopping the frosty Ninya from binding the land in ice.
Mathinnas People by Nan Chauncy, Oxford paperback. The fate of the Tasmanians told in fictional form.
Walkabout by James Vance Marshall. Two children, after an air crash, are rescued by an Aboriginal boy.
The Rocks of Honey by Patricia Wrightson (Puffin): the friendship between a white and an Aboriginal boy.

For adults:
The Australian Aboriginal Heritage by L. Berndt and E. Phillips (Ure-Smith) is a presentation of Aboriginal arts, a huge illustrated book, set of slides and record of songs, useful for schools.
The Remote Aborigines by C. Rowley (Penguin).
Outcasts in White Society by C. Rowley (Penguin).
Destruction of Aboriginal Society by C. Rowley (Penguin).

Important dates

40,000 BC or earlier Aborigines arrive in Australia.
1688 William Dampier met the Aborigines.
1770 Captain Cook hoisted the British flag at Botany Bay.
1820s Start of sheep-farming and movement of settlers over Australia.
1938 Settlers massacred 50 Aborigines at Myall Creek, New South Wales: seven of the settlers were hanged.
1890s–1950s The Australian Government set up large Aboriginal reserves on land not otherwise wanted.
1972 Aboriginal protesters put up a tent "Embassy" in Canberra.
1976 A referendum vote gave the federal government power to pass laws on Aboriginal affairs in all States, and included Aborigines in the census.
1978 *Aboriginal Land Rights (Northern Territory) Act (1976)* became effective. Aboriginal groups gained title under Australian law over 100,000 square miles of land in the Northern Territory.

47

Index